# Take up
# Snooker

## Take up Sport

Titles in this series currently available or shortly to be published:

# Take up Snooker

Principal contributor:

## Philip Yates

Philip Yates is a reporter with *Snooker Scene*, the game's leading magazine.

SPRINGFIELD BOOKS LIMITED

Copyright © Springfield Books Limited and White Line Press
1989

ISBN 0 947655 61 1

First published 1989 by
**Springfield Books Limited**
Springfield House, Norman Road, Denby Dale, Huddersfield
HD8 8TH

Reprinted 1991

Edited, designed and produced by
**White Line Press**
60 Bradford Road, Stanningley, Leeds LS28 6EF

Editors: Noel Whittall and Philip Gardner
Design: Krystyna Hewitt
Diagrams: Chris Oxlade

Printed and bound in Hong Kong

**Photographic credits**
Cover photograph: Action Plus
Thames Television: page 7
All other photographs by John Hipkiss, Eric Whitehead and
    John Hawken.

**Author's note on illustrations**
The instructional photographs are chiefly of Roger Bales, a
professional since 1984, who stood sixtieth in the world
rankings at the end of the 1987–88 season.

The Buskin brothers — Daniel, 12, and David, 13 — two of
the most promising young players in the country, also figure
in some of these pictures.

The photography sessions for this book were conducted at
Dudley Snooker Centre by courtesy of its proprietor, Graham
Morris.

# Contents

# 1

# Introduction

Snooker is a fascinating game with immense popular appeal — seven million regular players in Britain alone! It is also a game of skill and accuracy which requires lots of practice and patience before you begin to play well and win often.

This book cannot make you an expert, but it does explain the basics and provides a good introduction for newcomers to the game. Many of the terms used to describe snooker are familiar to everybody, but some may be new to you. They are all explained in chapter 11.

## A short history

In 1875, a group of British officers based in India, at the town now called Jabalpur, grew tired of playing billiards. Instead they devised an interesting alternative, which owed a little to both billiards and croquet. In its final form, a number of red balls were arranged on the table in a pyramid pattern, and six coloured balls were also introduced. After many enjoyable hours, someone jokingly called it "snooker", a slang expression for a young army recruit at the time, and the name has stuck ever since.

At first snooker was not taken too seriously, often being played only as an alternative to the better-established sport of billiards. However, as the years went by, snooker increased in popularity. In 1916, the first English Amateur Championship was held, and eleven years later the great Joe Davis organised and won the first ever World Professional Championship. Joe held on to the title for twenty years until he retired in 1947, and it was during this period that snooker overtook billiards in popularity.

In the 1950s and 60s, partly due to Joe's retirement, professional snooker looked in danger of extinction. Indeed, between 1958 and 1964 the world championship was not held. There was a similar lack of interest at grass-roots level, and during this period many clubs got rid of their tables.

The game's revival began in Britain in 1969. BBC2, then a relatively new television channel, decided that snooker was ideal for TV coverage and started a series called "Pot Black". The response to the new programme was fantastic. More and more people became interested in this colourful sport, and viewing figures continued to increase. In 1985, when Dennis Taylor defeated Steve Davis in the final frame to become world champion, no less than 18.5 million people watched the action live on TV. This exposure has led to prize money in the professional game rising to enormous levels, and the top players have become household names.

The amateur game is also going through a boom period. As well as the hundreds of local leagues and competitions, the Billiards and Snooker Control Council organises national amateur championships, including events for juniors.

More and more women are also becoming involved in what was once a male-dominated sport. There is an active governing body, the *World Ladies Billiards and Snooker Association*, which runs women's tournaments.

Snooker is rapidly becoming a truly worldwide sport. It is now played with enthusiasm in such varied locations as Ghana, Iceland, Hong Kong, Sweden and the United States of America.

All this adds up to make today the most exciting time ever to take up snooker.

*Joe Davis (right), World Champion for twenty years, is greeted by Ray Reardon on the television programme* This is Your Life.

# 2

# The game

Snooker is played on a standard billiard table (see page 14), using 22 balls. There are 15 reds, 6 colours and a white, which is known as the *cue ball*. The balls carry various point values, and the object of the game is to score more points than your opponent, both by correctly potting the balls into the pockets around the table, and by collecting penalty points when your opponent makes foul strokes. The red and coloured balls can be potted into any of the pockets, but the white ball must remain on the table.

At the beginning of each game, the reds are put into place using a triangular frame. Consequently, a single game of snooker has become known as a "frame", and matches are made up of a suitable number of frames. For example, the final of the World Professional Championship is contested over the best of 35 frames, but amateur events tend to be to the best of either five or seven frames.

## Striking the ball

The only ball which the cue is allowed to touch is the white. It must be struck cleanly with the tip of the cue — not pushed. For a stroke to be fair, the following conditions must apply:

● All the balls must be at rest

● The cue ball must only be hit once

● The striker must be touching the ground with at least one foot

● The striker must not touch any ball other than the white

● No balls may be forced off the table

You usually decide who makes the first stroke by tossing a coin. *Don't* flip the coin over the table, as it may damage the cloth if it drops onto it.

# The rules of play

At the beginning of a frame the balls are set out as shown in Figure 1. The first player places the white cue ball in the "D" and then hits it into the pyramid of reds. This is known as the "break-off" (see Figure 1). If a red is potted, one point is scored, and the player is entitled to attempt to pot a colour. If a colour is potted, the same player can attempt to pot another red, and so on, alternating reds and colours. Each player stays at the table until he or she either fails to pot a ball which is *on* (see panel) or commits a foul. When this happens, the score for that visit to the table (the break) is added to the scoreboard, and the other player's turn starts.

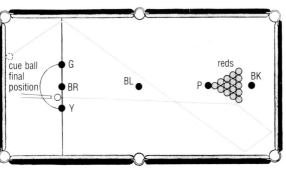

**Figure 1** How the balls are set up to start play. The white ball may be placed anywhere within the "D". The path shows a typical break-off (see chapter 9).

The red balls stay in the pocket once they have been potted, but the colours are replaced on the table on their designated spots. While there are any reds left on the table, the colours can be potted in any order, but once all fifteen reds have disappeared, the colours have to be potted in ascending numerical order: yellow, green, brown, blue, pink and, finally, black. When the black is potted, it is the end of the frame, and the player with the most points is the winner. If, however,

**Table 1** Score values

| Ball | Score |
|------|-------|
| Red | 1 |
| Yellow | 2 |
| Green | 3 |
| Brown | 4 |
| Blue | 5 |
| Pink | 6 |
| Black | 7 |

the scores are tied at this point, the black ball is re-spotted and play continues until either it is potted or one of the players makes a foul stroke.

---

### The ball "on"

In snooker, the order in which the balls can be potted is an important feature of the game. A ball is said to be "on" if it can legitimately be potted during the stroke being attempted — whether it is *possible* to pot it doesn't change the situation.

At the start of a frame, all fifteen reds are "on", and as each is potted you can choose any colour you like to follow it. You have to indicate to the referee — or to the other player in a friendly match — which colour you have selected, and the ball chosen becomes the one "on". This is called "nominating a colour". The last colour you can nominate is the one potted after the final red. Once it is replaced on the table, the colours come "on" according to value, from yellow through to black.

It is an offence for the cue ball to touch any other ball *before* it has struck one which is "on".

It is worth developing the habit of nominating a colour clearly: if you fail to, and then make a foul stroke, the penalty is automatically seven points, because it is assumed that you were going for the black!

---

### Foul strokes

As well as scoring by potting balls, you can gain points if your opponent makes a so-called foul stroke. The minimum penalty for this is four points. If the blue, pink or black balls are involved, the penalty will be five, six or seven points respectively. Much of the skill (and frustration) in snooker centres around foul strokes and forced errors.

The three most common foul shots for which penalty points are awarded are:

● failure to hit the object ball

● pocketing the cue ball, known as an "in-off"

● hitting the wrong ball, for example a red when aiming for one of the other colours.

Other foul shots, which occur less frequently, include striking a ball while others are still moving, playing a shot with both feet off the ground, and touching a ball with your clothing.

### The snooker

Most of the fouls listed above are accidental errors. However, the first one is the exception: you can often force your opponent to miss the object ball by "laying a snooker". A typical example occurs when a player has to hit a red, but is left with the cue ball in such a position that coloured balls are in the way, and make a direct strike impossible. In this situation, the player is said to be "snookered". Contact with the red can only be made by bouncing the cue ball off the cushions or by playing a swerve shot, and the risk of missing it is high. Snookers can occur on any ball, and it is also quite possible to snooker yourself by accident!

### Problems with spotting colours

When a colour which has been potted cannot be replaced because its spot is occupied by another ball, it is placed on the highest-value spot available. Sometimes all six spots are occupied, in which case the colour is placed as near as possible to its own spot, in a direct line with the top cushion.

### Touching ball

If the cue ball comes to rest touching another ball, the player has no option but to play the cue ball away, without moving the touching ball. If you fail to play away you are considered to have made a push stroke. Provided that the ball the white touches is nominated as the ball "on", the white can be "played away" without penalty: it does not have to hit any other ball. Take care: if the touching ball moves at all, it counts as a push stroke.

### Push stroke

As the name suggests, this occurs when the cue stays in contact with the white ball after it has started moving. Push strokes most commonly occur when cue ball and object ball are very close together.

### Free ball

If you are snookered as a result of a foul shot, you are allowed to play for any colour you nominate. For instance, if you are unable to hit any of the reds, but the black is attractively positioned, you can nominate the black, which for the purposes of that shot is treated as a red and counts one point if potted. However, in such circumstances the black is replaced on its spot, whereas a "real" red would remain in the pocket.

### The play-again rule

If you find yourself in an awkward position after your opponent has played a foul stroke, you are entitled to ask your opponent to play again.

## The jump shot

Years ago, players were allowed to jump the white over an intervening ball. This was always a risky business, and is now illegal, although if a ball hops into the air *after* the cue ball has contacted the object ball, no foul has been committed.

## Scoring

Develop the habit of putting your score on the board at the end of each break — it is far too easy to forget where you are if you do it after each stroke. If you commit a foul, its value is added to your opponent's score, not taken away from yours.

## The full rules

The rules of snooker can be complex, and even the most experienced players do not usually claim to know them all. This summary will enable you to play a fair game and to cope with most situations, but the full rules can be easily obtained from the Billiards and Snooker Control Council (see page 48).

# 3

# The equipment

## Cues, tips and chalk

The rules of the game require you to play with a cue which is at least 3 feet (910 mm) long. One which reaches to approximately 2½ inches (60 mm) below your shoulder level and weighs between 16 and 18 ounces (450–500 g) will probably be about right for you. These are only guidelines: the optimum length and weight largely depend on your physical characteristics and personal preference. Only you can decide whether you are comfortable with a particular cue and feel that you will be able to play to your full potential with it. Youngsters are often put off the game because they find a full-size cue difficult and awkward to use. Growing children will usually do best if they start off with a short cue which is replaced by a longer one from time to time.

The best cues are made of maple or ash. Nowadays the two-piece cue which joins together in the middle has become popular. Over the years these cues have been refined to the point where Steve Davis and Jimmy White use them. The great advantage of two-piece cues is that they are easily transportable without damage.

Always maintain your cue — keep it clean by giving it an occasional wipe with a barely-damp cloth and treat it as a friend. Remember, if you reach a respectable standard and then lose your cue through breakage or theft, your game will surely suffer.

Once the cue has been selected, the next consideration is that its tip is up to standard. The best tips are *Elk Master* or *Blue Diamond*. When choosing one, bear in mind that it should be neither too hard nor too soft. A hard tip will tend to skid off the ball and make it difficult to control, while soft or spongy ones make it hard to judge the strength for a shot.

When in place, a tip should be gently domed with a file to give maximum responsiveness.

It is also important to chalk the tip regularly while playing, so as to make a miscue less likely. Most knowledgeable players use either *National Tournament* or *Triangle* chalks, both of which are made in the USA. Professionals prefer green chalk because it does not stick to the cue ball, as blue chalk sometimes does.

---

# The table and its accessories

A snooker table has a level *bed* made of two-inch-thick slate, *cushions* made of rubber, and a *cloth surface* made from blended wools. The table can be built to either imperial or metric standards, but cannot be a mixture of the two. Imperial full-size tables have a playing area of 11 ft 8½ in x 5 ft 10 in, measured *inside* the cushion faces. The metric version is 3.5 m x 1.75 m. The pockets have to conform to the templates issued by the BSCC. The height has to be between 2 ft 9½in and 2 ft 10½ in (850 mm to 875 mm). The cloth is always green to look like grass – a reflection of the croquet influence of the early days.

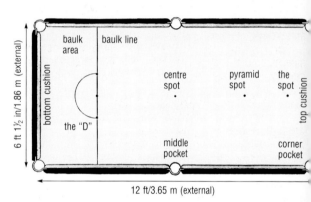

**Figure 2** The main features of the table

All matches and official competitions are played on these full-size tables, but tables of smaller dimensions such as 6 ft x 3 ft (1.8 m x 0.9 m) or 8 ft x 4 ft (2.4 m x 1.2 m) can provide an ideal introduction into the game for a young player.

### Rests
Rests are accessories which help players to reach shots which they could not otherwise attempt. They are approximately 5 ft (1.5 m) long and have an X-shaped head usually made of plastic or steel. This head holds the cue in position while a shot is being played, thus taking the place of the player's hand on the table.

Special rests such as the *half butt* and *spider* are available for particularly awkward shots (see chapter 8).

### Balls

Originally, snooker balls were made from wood or ivory, but nowadays a resin compound is used. Each ball is $2\frac{1}{16}$ inches in diameter, and there must be no more than three grams difference between the individual balls in each set. The most popular types today are *Super Crystalate* and *Aramith*, which are more responsive to spin, screw and stun shots than previous ones. This has made controlling the cue ball and building a break easier than it has ever been.

# Clothing

No special clothing is needed for snooker, but you should always take a pride in your appearance. Only professionals have to wear dress suits to play, but many clubs discourage certain types of attire: the Billiards and Snooker Control Council does not allow competitors to wear denims or training shoes in the English Amateur Championships. Anyway, the old adage "If you look good, you feel good" applies in snooker as it does in most other sports.

For obvious reasons, avoid anything with baggy sleeves which may touch balls you are attempting to cue over; slippery shoes are not a good idea either!

# Where to learn

Although miniature tables provide a good start, after a while you need to play on a full-size table. It is not usually practicable to have such a table at home, so the best solution is generally to join a snooker club.

Today, virtually every town has a purpose-built snooker centre which offers facilities such as coaching and in-house competitions, both of which are ideal for beginners. There will also be the opportunity to join teams which are entered in local leagues. In addition, the general environment in these clubs promotes good snooker. This is often aided by the presence of high-grade players who use such clubs as practice bases.

Many clubs make special efforts to attract junior members, and players of all levels of ability are welcomed. The large number of teenagers playing the game at a very high level is mainly due to the excellent facilities which are available nowadays.

In Britain, the Billiards and Snooker Foundation provides coaching for young players; it is at the same address as the Billiards and Snooker Control Council (see page 48).

# 4

# The basics

## Grip

Ideally, the cue should be held a few inches from the end of the butt (as in photo 1). It should be held with enough strength to keep it horizontal without any other support. If you hold the cue lightly with the tips of the fingers, as many billiards players in the past used to do, certain shots such as *stun* and *screw* become difficult to play. Don't grip too tightly either: a hard or fierce grip tends to produce tension, which leads to a loss of fluency.

*Hold the cue a few inches from the end of the butt.*

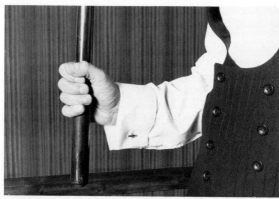

What you need is a firm grip, with four fingers wrapped around the butt of the cue (photo 2). While your hold on the cue should be firm enough to enable you to keep it under control, in the end the exact strength of your grip will depend largely on what you feel really comfortable with. The right amount of firmness will stop your wrist from becoming floppy, and will ensure that the stroke is made with forearm, wrist, hand and cue all working together (photo 3).

*All four fingers should be around the butt.*

*The grip should be positive: make sure that your wrist stays firm.*

## Bridge

Once you are holding the cue correctly, the next step is to be able to make a bridge with the other hand. The bridge is vital because it holds your stance firm: it acts as the front leg of a tripod, the other two parts of which are your legs. Despite its obvious importance, many people play with a poor bridge all their lives, and their progress is limited as a result.

The way to make an effective bridge is simple. First, lay your hand on the cloth, spread your fingers wide and then stretch them until they become taut. Now pull the finger pads inwards, and see how your hand becomes raised off the table in a slight hump (photo 4). Your bridge hand is now resting on its heel, fingertips and the underpart of the thumb.

To complete the bridge, cock your thumb high, forming a channel between fingers and thumb which will allow the cue to move through it when the shot is played (see photo 5). Make sure that this channel is not too wide, or you will find it virtually impossible to stop the cue wobbling from side to side.

*A good bridge. See how pulling the finger pads inwards has raised the hand in a slight hump.*

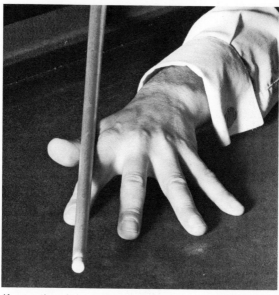

*If your thumb is cocked well up, the cue will have a natural channel in which to travel.*

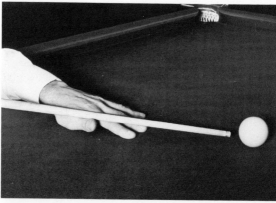

*Your bridge hand should be 7 or 8 inches (18–20 cm) from the ball.*

If you remember to grip the cloth strongly with the pads of your fingers and to keep your bridge arm thrust out as straight as possible, you will find that the bridge hand becomes almost immovable. This will allow you to keep still while playing a shot and also make it easier for you to line up correctly. For most people the optimum distance from the bridge hand to the cue ball is between seven and eight inches (180–200 mm) (see photo 6). Note, though, that taller players need to bend the bridge arm to avoid "standing off" the cue ball and being unable to follow through properly.

The standard bridge needs space on the table for your hand, and you will often meet awkward positions when it cannot be used. The most common of these is when the cue ball is close to the cushion. When you find yourself in this position, make a *cushion bridge* (see photo 7) by placing four fingers on the wooden part of the cushion rail and dropping your wrist slightly below it. Despite the fact that the cue is running over the cushion rail, you will feel more comfortable and less restricted than if you attempt to place your hand on the cloth.

Another situation which tends to terrify novices arises when it is necessary to bridge over intervening balls. With a makeshift bridge, beginners tend to hurry the shot and often make mistakes as a result. The best advice is to keep calm, try to get at least two finger pads on the cloth, and never try anything fancy! (See photos 8 and 9).

## Stance

After you have developed your grip and bridge, you complete the basics by getting your stance right.

Your front leg (the left if you are right-handed) should be bent and must take most of your weight, with the foot pointing in the direction of the shot. Your back leg should be straight and rigid, with the foot turned out just enough to provide maximum stability (photo 10). Don't let your chest become too square-on to the shot.

*Form a cushion bridge by placing four fingers on the wooden part of the cushion rail and dropping your wrist slightly below it.*

The position of your feet plays an important part in keeping your body still as the shot is made. However, there is no hard and fast rule as to how far apart they should be. This largely depends upon your height and what you feel comfortable with. You should be trying to make the cue run as horizontally as possible, and it should lightly brush your chin and chest, both of which act as additional aids to keep it in line.

The important thing to remember is that your stance must work naturally for *you*. Don't try consciously to keep in a certain position if this affects your rhythm and timing, as both are crucial for good snooker.

*When bridging over intervening balls, always try to form as solid a bridge as possible, with at least two fingers on the cloth.*

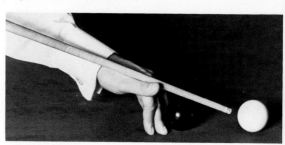

**10**

*A good stance: the back leg is rigid for maximum stability.*

# 5

# Playing the shot

When you have achieved a sound grip, bridge and stance, the next step is to learn how and where to strike the cue ball. You will do best if your delivery is straight and your alignment accurate. Therefore, the development of a sound cue action and the ability to sight the shot properly are vitally important for anyone attempting to play good snooker.

## Sighting

Snooker is a game of minute fractions, so the importance of correct sighting cannot be overstated. The orthodox advice for sighting is that the cue should brush the chin directly below the nose so that both eyes can fully concentrate on the shot in hand (see photo 11).

However, this method does not work if a player happens to have one eye stronger than the other. Many great players, including Joe Davis, have had a weak right eye, and this has caused them to run the cue directly under their left eye. Like them, you should always cue under what is known as your "master eye".

---

**Finding your master eye**

If you are in any doubt about which of your eyes is the master, try these simple tests:

- With both eyes open, hold a pencil vertical, at arm's length, and line it up with a corner of the room. Now close each eye in turn. When you close your master eye, the pencil seems to move out of alignment.

- Use the pencil to make a hole in the middle of a sheet of paper. Again keeping both eyes open, sight through the hole to any distant object. If you steadily bring the paper back to your face while keeping the object in view, the hole will end up at your master eye.

---

*David Buskin sights naturally with his left eye.*

Assuming your alignment is correct, you are now fully equipped to strike the cue ball, so remember that your actions before the shot will have a direct influence on it. Before hitting the white, line up your cue and make a number of preliminary short strokes which are smooth and rhythmical but do not quite touch the ball. This is called "addressing the ball"; it builds up your concentration and steadies you for the shot to come.

Also, look at both the cue ball and the object ball several times before the shot, moving only your eyes, not your head. If you are trying to pot a black, you should be looking at the black as the shot is made. When you strike the cue ball, you should be looking at where contact will be made on the object ball.

## Cue action

Your elbow is a hinge, and the cue action is a simple movement of opening and closing it. The cue is drawn back as the hinge opens, and pushed forward as it closes. You must not let the hinge twist at all during the stroke. The movement of your forearm should be the *only* thing that pushes the cue through, not your shoulders or any other part of the upper body (see photo 12).

*The cue drawn back: it will be pushed forward using the forearm only. There should be no movement of the shoulders or any other part of the body.*

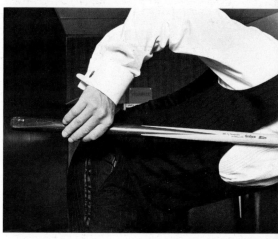

Novices often cannot wait to find out how the shot has finished, and so look up before the stroke has been completed. This is a basic fault, as it causes a loss of straightness in the delivery which leads to mistakes being made. If you take a close look at an ace player such as Steve Davis, you will see how his head and upper body stay down over the ball long after the shot has been made.

Another part of the cue action in which faults are common is the backswing. Ideally, the cue should be taken back smoothly, pause for a fraction of a second at the end of the backswing, then come "through" the ball, clean and straight. Never draw the cue back too much or allow it to move in short disjointed jerks.

The stroke should finish with the cue dead on line. It should strike through the ball for several inches and then stop exactly in the same "groove". If this is achieved, the object ball will go precisely where it was aimed. The backswing and follow-through needed for a shot of medium strength are shown in photos 13, 14 and 15.

Once you have developed a reasonable cue action, you should still continue to experiment and make adjustments accordingly. Even the top professionals can gain from minor technical alterations.

Differences in physical make-up and development mean that there are as many different cue actions as there are players. Ultimately, you must evolve your own method and style. Find out what works best for *you*: don't try to be a carbon copy of your snooker hero.

*The movement of the cue from backswing to follow-through. The whole action must be smooth.*

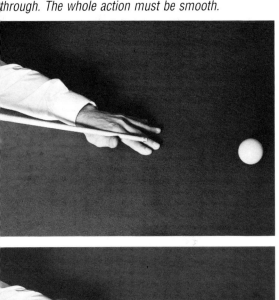

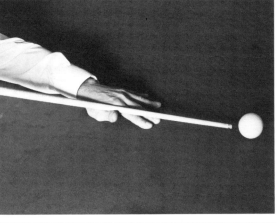

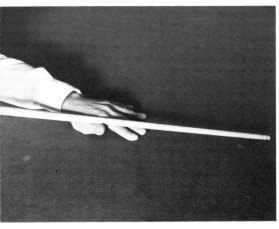

# 6

## How to pot

When a solid and workable cue action has been developed and you are striking the cue ball well, the next step is to learn about potting. This is the most important part of the game, and consistent potting is essential if you are to be at all successful. Until you can pot well enough to construct breaks of a reasonable length, there is little chance that you will win many frames.

At the novice stage, it is tempting to try to force things along by trying to combine potting with complicated positional play, but this is the wrong approach. The development of your game should be taken one step at a time, and you should master the art of potting before you become much concerned with positional play (see chapter 7).

Always remember that the margin for error when attempting to pot anything other than a ball sitting over a pocket is extremely small. Throughout your play, the principles of straight cueing and lack of body movement must be maintained.

## Theory of potting

The theory of potting is simple enough to understand, if not always so easy to put into practice. Basically, the object ball is propelled towards its target, the pocket, by the cue ball striking it in a particular way. Beginners often find they get problems with the straight pot (Figure 3), but in fact it is not a difficult shot. The cue ball must simply make what is known as a *full-ball* contact with the object ball in order to send it towards the pocket.

Obviously, the vast majority of pots are not straight, but require the object ball to be sent off at an angle. Figure 4 shows a position where, to pot the pink, a half-ball contact is needed; in other words, the cue ball will have to cover half of the object ball at the moment of impact.

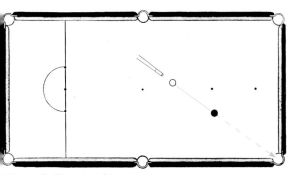

**Figure 3** The straight pot

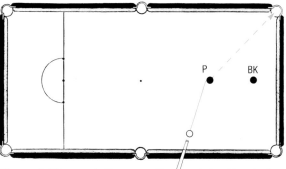

**Figure 4** The cue ball must strike the pink with a half-ball contact if the pot is to be successful.

If, for example, the white strikes the pink with less than half-ball contact (say, quarter-ball), the pot will be missed because the pink will have been hit too "thinly". In this case the attempted pot is said to be "overcut". If the pink is struck too full, the term used is "undercut"; the object ball will again miss the pocket, but on the opposite side.

While the basics of potting can be explained in this way, you will not be able to appreciate the subtleties of how to pot well without the benefit of some experience on the table. Initially, your lack of knowledge will lead to easy pots being missed even though you may have developed the most orthodox and effective cue action imaginable. It simply takes time to learn where the object ball should be hit to make a particular pot.

This inability to pot often leads to confusion and frustration, but do persevere! After a while things become clearer, and you will no longer consciously have to compute angles. Play as frequently as you can, and soon you will get the balls in the pockets instinctively, having learned from experience what type of contact is needed.

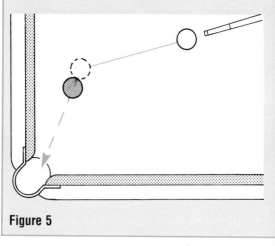

**Figure 5**

No matter how much you practise, you will never become perfect at potting. Even the greats of the game can miss occasionally, despite their fanatical dedication. However, if you want to improve your potting skills, you will find that there is no substitute for practice. Everyone goes through this learning process, and it is undoubtedly the only path to good potting and thus to successful snooker.

## Playing conditions

As full-size snooker tables are all of similar size, and the game is played indoors, free from the influences of the weather, you could be forgiven for thinking that playing conditions do not vary greatly. Wrong!

Any experienced campaigner can tell many stories about the idiosyncrasies of certain tables, such as strange reactions off the cushions, uneven slates, odd pockets, and, most commonly, the state of the cloth itself.

Sometimes the problems are obvious — a badly maintained table may have cigarette burns, beer stains and bald patches. However, even tables which appear sound can produce hidden surprises: if a cloth is too heavy, for example, the balls will be slow in running, whereas if it is too smooth, the balls will travel further and will be difficult to control.

> **Understanding the nap**
> The nap of the cloth is similar to the grain in a piece of wood. It always runs from the baulk end of the table towards the top cushion. The path of a ball which is hit parallel to the side cushions and without any "side" will not be affected by the nap. However, such a shot is quite rare, so you need to get a feel for the way the nap can affect the run of your shots.
>     The effect is most critical when trying to make slow pots into the middle pockets: if you make the shot from the baulk end, the ball will be running "with the grain", and will tend to overshoot slightly, drifting towards the far jaw of the pocket. If a similar shot is made from the top cushion, the ball will "pull in" a little towards the near jaw (Figure 6).

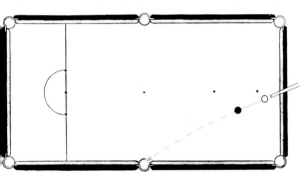

**Figure 6** A shot towards the middle pocket from the top cushion will pull in towards the near jaw.

### Other variables
The speed a ball comes off the cushion, the tightness of the pockets, and the response of the balls to particular types of shot, are other variables a player has to take into account when playing on a strange table.

Try to develop some very simple practice routines which you use *every time* you get the opportunity to play on a table which is new to you. It will not be long before you develop the skill of judging how a table will "play" — a skill which will often give you a winning edge when you take part in leagues and tournaments.

# 7

# Shots and spin

At first you will be happy just to get the right ball into a pocket, but soon you will discover that positioning the cue ball for the next shots is a vital part of the game. If you are to play successful and skilful snooker, this ability to control the cue ball is a must. The modern game revolves around leaving it in a position which makes the next shot easy for you – or, if need be, hard for your opponent. The better you become at controlling the white, the easier you will find it to build high-scoring breaks.

## Positional play
Positional play requires you to control both the object ball and the cue ball. This two-ball control can be very difficult for a novice, as this simple exercise will show: place the blue on its spot and the cue ball midway between the blue and one of the middle pockets. You will find that potting the blue into the other middle pocket is child's play. Now try the same pot, but making the cue ball screw back twelve inches, and you will find that your failure rate will increase considerably.

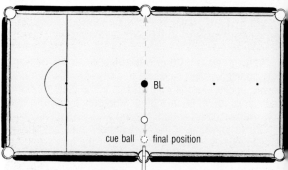

**Figure 7** See if you can retain potting accuracy when screwing back the cue ball.

Cue-ball control is achieved through using different forms of spin which are generated by striking the cue ball at different points on its surface. The three main types of spin are *topspin*, *backspin* and *sidespin*.

## Topspin

Think of the cue ball as representing a clock face: if the cue strikes it at twelve o'clock, you will generate lots of topspin (see photo 16). This will cause the cue ball to follow through after it has made contact with the object ball. Coming down from twelve o'clock, as you strike the cue ball closer to its centre, you will produce less spin and correspondingly less follow-through.

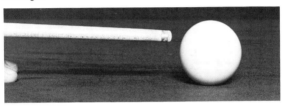

## Backspin

Conversely, striking *below* centre will put backspin on the cue ball. This causes it to stop dead or even roll backwards when it hits the object ball.

If you strike just a little below centre, the small amount of backspin will make the white stop dead if it hits the object ball squarely: this is called a *stun* (see photo 17).

As you strike further down the ball, more backspin is produced. This causes the cue ball to come back towards you after it has made contact with the object ball. This is called a *screw shot* (see photo 18).

Beginners often marvel at how the top professionals achieve powerful screw shots, but in reality they are fairly simple. The most common mistake made by novices is to use their normal bridge when attempting to play the shot. This will cause you to strike down on the ball, which leads to a loss of spin and also decreases potting accuracy.

To remedy this, lower your bridge so that the cue runs as horizontally as possible when striking the cue ball. This is simple enough to perfect, as photo 19 shows.

It is also important to remember to let your cue do the work. Always follow through so that you can sense the tip of the cue as it hits the cue ball. Although screw shots require power, you must resist the temptation to put your shoulder and upper body behind them. Instead, cue smoothly, just as you would with a normal shot. Getting this right is vital, for screw shots are needed in virtually every frame of snooker.

## Sidespin

The third and final type of spin which you can apply to the cue ball is sidespin, known simply as *side*. If the white is hit on its right-hand side (i.e. the tip strikes the ball at three o'clock), the ball is initially pushed to the left (see photo 20). However, as the spin bites, the ball will curve back to the right.

Side is mainly used to aid positional play, which it does by altering the natural angle at which the cue ball leaves the cushion. From a given position, striking the white on one side will *widen* the angle it takes off the cushion; this is called *running side*. Striking the white on the opposite side will narrow the angle; this is called *check side*.

Side is undoubtedly the most difficult form of spin to master, and even the most experienced players sometimes find its use baffling. Perhaps the most sensible advice that can be given to someone just taking up the game is this: *understand the basic principle, practise its application, but only attempt to use side when there is no alternative!*

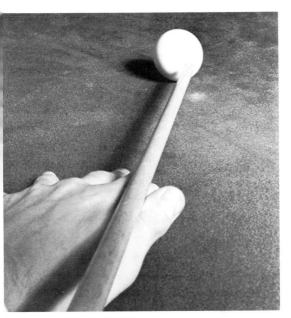

*Striking the ball for "side"*

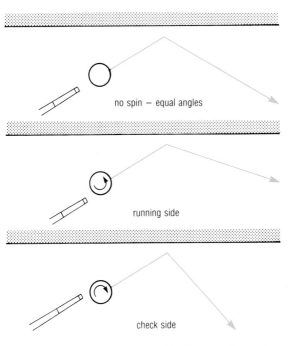

**Figure 8** Sidespin has a powerful effect on the angle with which the cue ball rebounds from the cushion.

# 8

## Using
## the rest

When the cue ball stops in certain positions, it is sometimes impossible to reach the shot with your normal bridge. This is when you must use the rest.

Some of the great players in snooker history, including world champions Joe Davis and John Spencer, have been less than happy when using the rest. Many amateurs never master it, but do not let this put you off: it is really not difficult to use correctly.

Most beginners play with the rest "tall way up", but this is the wrong approach unless you need to strike high on the cue ball. The shallow vee should be used for the vast majority of shots, because it allows the cue to strike the white dead centre (see photo 21).

The grip to use when playing with the rest is radically different from the orthodox grip used in normal situations. The cue should be held at the end of the butt, rather like a pen (see photo 22). Two fingers are placed on top, and the thumb underneath: it is your thumb which controls the power needed to play the shot. Use your other hand to anchor the rest to the table, as any movement will inevitably produce errors.

*Roger Bales shows the pen-like grip used for shots with the rest.*

The cue must be held just below eye level, so that it is possible to sight the stroke correctly along the length of the cue. As you are now side-on to the ball, your cue action becomes basically a push with the wrist and forearm (see photo 23). Note how the shot is completed with your forearm horizontal. It is difficult at first to cue straight when using this method, but eventually, with plenty of practice, you will find it almost as easy as with the normal bridge.

As with your normal action, it is vitally important to develop a smooth rhythm. Make a few preliminary addresses at the cue ball before playing the shot, and throughout the stroke keep movement to an absolute minimum.

Beware of trying to do too much with the white when using the rest: keep the shots simple. Obviously you cannot lower the rest head for a screw shot as you can with your normal bridge, so a downward blow has to be struck instead of a horizontal one. This increases the risk of a miscue, so it is not advisable to attempt deep screw shots with the rest.

Apart from the standard rest, there are other implements which help you to play certain awkward shots.

The *half butt* is a long rest measuring about nine feet (2.8 metres) overall. It is used solely for shots where a player has to reach almost the whole length of the table, and always comes complete with a matching cue. However, these long cues have now almost become redundant, as most regular players use cue extensions. These are an ingenious development which allows you to use your own cue with the half butt, and they have naturally become very popular as a result.

*The action is a push with the wrist and forearm.*

The rest used for high bridging is called a *spider*. It allows you to cue over any intervening balls which would obstruct the normal rest. As with the ordinary rest, the spider should be anchored to the bed of the table with your free hand (see photo 24). Never attempt a complicated shot with the spider, because it forces you to hit down onto the cue ball, and this means that almost anything can happen: even the most elementary pots can be missed.

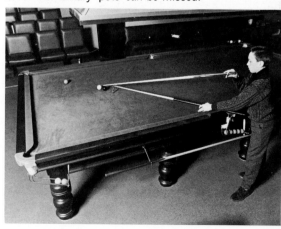

Although playing with the rest is sometimes difficult to begin with, do persevere — in the long run it pays to learn to use it confidently. Because children have a short reach, they have to use the rest for a high proportion of shots, and quickly get used to it. Many older novices are frightened of it, however, and end up contorting their bodies in order to reach the shot. This is bad, as overstretching leads to many mistakes owing to poor alignment.

*Twelve-year-old Daniel Buskin is at home with the rest.*

# 9

## Match tactics

Tactical awareness, like good potting and positional play, must be an integral part of your snooker armoury.

## Safety play

Safety play is the art of leaving the cue ball in a position where it will not give the other player an easy shot.

There are two distinct forms of safety — *aggressive* and *negative*. In playing the former, you actively try to place your opponent in a difficult situation, while a negative safety shot merely stops him or her from scoring. Take care with negative safety — it often allows your opponent to play a good safety shot in return, and thus seize the initiative. Therefore, negative safety shots should only be played when there is no alternative.

### At the start of a frame

If you watch a snooker match between players of any standard, you will see that in the opening exchanges

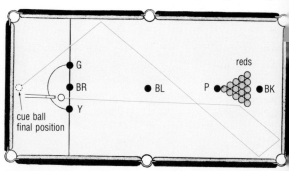

**Figure 9** The most popular opening shot. The cue ball is brought back down the table so that the next shot is very difficult for your opponent.

**Figure 10** If you are not confident of potting one of the reds, use a safety shot which leaves the cue ball as far from them as possible.

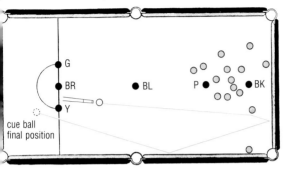

of virtually every frame both players concentrate on bringing the cue ball back into baulk so that their opponent is not left with a simple potting opportunity (see Figures 9 and 10).

In this situation, do not just go through the motions of leaving the cue ball in the baulk area. Instead think clearly, study the positions of the balls, and then, by visualising the completed shot, try to place the cue ball so that your rival is in the most awkward spot possible (see Figure 11).

If you are certain that you will not leave a possible pot after playing a particular safety shot, try to split up the reds as much as you can. By doing this, you are increasing your potential potting opportunities should your opponent make a mistake.

Likewise, always be on the lookout for the chance to play a "shot to nothing". This is when you can attempt a pot, safe in the knowledge that, if you miss, the cue ball will run to safety (see Figure 12).

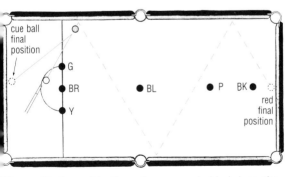

**Figure 11** A combination of screw and side brings the cue ball back onto the bottom cushion while the red ends up at the other end of the table.

**Figure 12** A screw shot to nothing. Potting the red into the top left-hand pocket is a long and difficult shot. If the cue ball is brought back to the baulk cushion, you can be confident that your opponent will not be left with an easy shot if you miss.

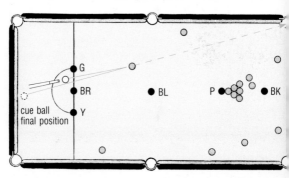

There are 21 balls on the table at the start of a frame, so the path of the cue ball back to a safe position is often blocked. Therefore, it is important to learn the "angles" of the table, so that safety routes can be correctly calculated.

### The double kiss

One of the possible consequences of an inaccurate shot is the "double kiss". This occurs when the cue ball and object ball make contact for a second time after they have struck a cushion. The effect is very unpredictable, and can completely change the pattern of the game. You cannot always avoid a double kiss, but do try to keep the possibility in mind when attempting a slightly risky shot. It may be wiser to try something else...

## The snooker

When only a few balls remain on the table and you are a few points behind, don't throw in the towel — you need a snooker. But don't feel you have to lay a snooker with every shot: just play safe until the chance to lay a snooker arrives. Often your opponent can be forced to try to escape from an outrageously difficult snooker; will fail, leave an easy pot and lose the frame as a result.

If you need a snooker to win, it is true that you are second favourite! However, remember these two points:

● By prolonging the frame, you can break your opponent's rhythm and cause a few anxious moments at the same time.

40

**Figure 13** Using the stun effect to leave a snooker. In this case the cue ball replaces the last red which had been just behind the black.

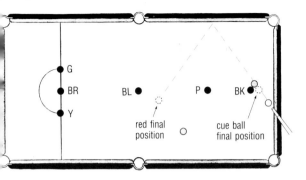

- If you do upset the odds and steal the frame, you get a major psychological boost and leave your rival demoralised and frustrated.

## A positive approach

Develop a positive approach to your matches. You can gain an advantage by taking some very simple steps:

- Always arrive at the venue with plenty of time to spare. A mad last-minute dash is bad, because it does not allow you to compose yourself before the start of the match.

- Never eat a big meal immediately before you play. Apart from dulling the senses, it often makes you feel more uncomfortable as nerves come into play.

When the match begins, it is best to concentrate on playing the balls, not your opponent. Never be intimidated by your rival, just play the shots you have learned in practice. If they go wrong, do not worry — it's all good match experience!

Throughout the match, concentrate on every shot and be determined. Think positively about winning, but above all enjoy yourself. Revel in the close games as well as the easy victories, learn from your mistakes and you will begin to look forward to every match.

# 10

# Practice routines

Solo practice is essential for novice and professional alike. Indeed, the top stars practise for up to six hours a day, honing their already finely-tuned skills. As a beginner, you probably won't have the time or the inclination to do this, but even a limited amount of solo work will hasten your improvement.

Always concentrate on each shot, and if you miss, try again. Because you are not under match pressure, you can experiment in an uninhibited way on the practice table.

## Checking the basics

There are two simple exercises which check whether you have got the basics right. The first of these is used by the well-known coach, Frank Callan, to test the effectiveness of a player's bridge. Set the cue ball on the baulk line and make a stroke directly along the line. If, after the stroke has been completed, the cue has drifted to the right of the line, it means that the thumb of your bridge hand is too low. If the cue drifts to the left, your thumb is too high and must be lowered.

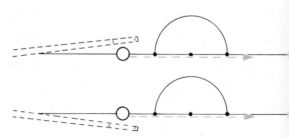

**Figure 14** Checking the bridge for a right-handed player. If the cue tip finishes to the left of the baulk line (*above*), your thumb is too high; if it finishes to the right (*below*), your thumb is too low.

The second exercise tests the straightness of your cue action. Place the cue ball on the brown spot, then aim it straight up the table so that its path goes over the blue, pink and black spots. If, on the return journey from the top cushion, the cue ball veers off to the left or right, you have problems (see photo 26).

*Check for cueing accuracy by sending the ball up the table over all the centre spots: it should pass over all of them again on the way back.*

If the ball strays away from the spots in this way, it is because you have given it some unintentional sidespin. This is almost certainly due to a poor stance, movement during the shot, or a combination of both. Work out what is going wrong so that the "side" can be eradicated, allowing the cue ball to follow a straight course.

## Potting practice

You will also need lots of potting practice. Set up potting situations which require different angles of contact, and with the ball at various distances from the pocket.

Identify the weakest parts of your game, and be sure to practise them. If you have difficulty in mastering one particular shot, keep setting it up. Practice pays off in time: eventually you will get it right.

### The line-up
Perhaps the most popular practice routine is known as the *line-up* (see photo 27). Put the colours on their normal spots and then place the reds in a straight line between them. The reds should be approximately two inches apart. The basic idea is simple: you must

*The line-up practice routine.*

attempt to compile a break in the normal way, red–colour–red, disturbing only the ball you are trying to pot. This exercise aids both potting and cue-ball control.

Practice is not boring if you keep a note of your best scores and set targets for yourself to aim at. When Steve Davis, the most dedicated of the modern players, was a young amateur he would not allow himself anything to eat or drink until he had cleared the table. Even if you don't reach these heights of self-denial, determined practice is vital if you are seriously interested in becoming a good exponent of the game. As in most sports, you get out of it what you put in. Success and skill do not come on a plate, but have to be worked for.

**Figure 15** A double (see facing page) is used here to pot the pink, as the obvious pocket is blocked by the black.

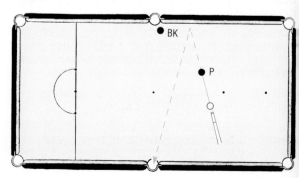

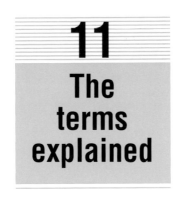

# 11
# The terms explained

**Angled** If the ball "on" cannot be hit directly because the cue ball is obstructed by the jaws of a pocket, the player is said to be *angled*.

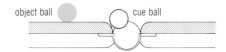

object ball    cue ball

**Figure 16** *Angled:* the ball "on" cannot be contacted because of the position of the jaws of the pocket.

**Baulk** The area of the table between the baulk line and the bottom cushion.

**Break** A sequence of scoring shots, and also the number of points scored from them.

**Break-off** The first shot of the frame.

**Clear the table** A break in which a player pots all the balls left on the table.

**Cue ball** The white ball: the only ball in snooker which is struck with the cue.

**D** The area of the table inside the semi-circle by the baulk line.

**Double** A shot where the object ball is potted after it has made contact with at least one cushion.

**Extension** A tubular extension which can be attached to the cue in order to lengthen it. It may be used with or without the half butt rest to reach awkwardly placed shots.

**Foul shot** An illegal stroke which results in penalty points being given away to your opponent.

**Frame** This is the name given to a single game. A match is made up of an agreed number of frames. The name comes from the triangular frame used to set up the red balls.

**Free ball** If you are snookered after a foul shot by an opponent, you may nominate any colour as a red. If it is potted, you score one point and then nominate a colour as usual. If all the reds have left the table, the free ball is valued at the same number of points as the lowest valued ball on the table, and the colours are then taken in sequence. Remember, you are snookered if there is no ball *on* which you can hit all parts of with a direct stroke.

**Full contact** This is when the cue ball hits the object ball in the dead centre as you look at it.

**In hand** The cue ball is *in hand* after it has either gone *in-off* or been forced off the table. It is placed in the D to re-start the game.

**In-off** If you pocket the cue ball after it has made contact with another object ball, it is said to have gone *in-off*.

**Jump shot** When the cue ball jumps over the object ball or any intervening ball. It is a foul stroke.

**Maximum break** This is a score of 147, achieved by potting 15 reds, 15 blacks and all the colours, in a single sequence.

**Object ball** The ball which the white is intended to hit.

**Pot** The act of playing the cue ball onto the object ball, so that it sends the object ball into a pocket.

**Plant** The simple plant is a shot involving three balls: the cue ball strikes the first ball, which in turn hits a second in such a way that the second ball is potted. More complex plants involving several balls are possible, but the results become difficult to control.

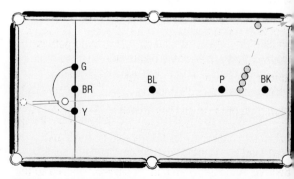

**Figure 17** A complex plant: worth a try, and nice if it comes off! In any case, if the stroke is made with just enough power to bring the cue ball back into baulk, the position should be left fairly safe.

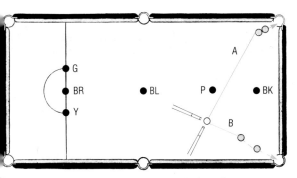

**Figure 18** Here the player has the choice of a set (shot A) or a plant (shot B).

**Push stroke** This occurs when the cue ball remains in contact with the tip of the cue after it has started moving forward. It is a foul shot.

**Safety shot** A shot from which a player does not intend to score but hopes to leave his opponent in a position from which a scoring strike is unlikely.

**Screw** This is backspin or reverse spin applied to the cue ball by hitting it well below centre. Hence a *screw shot* (see page 31).

**Set** Similar to a plant, but with two balls actually touching. This makes it possible to pot the second ball with virtually any angle of contact on the first.

**Shot to nothing** A shot in which a player attempts to pot a ball in such a way that if he is unsuccessful he is assured of leaving the cue ball in a safe position.

**Side** Sidespin applied to the cue ball by striking it either left or right of centre (see page 32).

**Snooker** Apart from being the name of the sport, a snooker is also a situation where the cue ball cannot hit all of the object ball directly because its path is blocked by an intervening ball or balls.

**Spider** An elevated rest used for awkward shots which require difficult bridging.

**Stun** A shot in which the cue ball stops dead on hitting the object ball. This only happens if the contact is *full*. Stun is achieved by striking the cue ball just below centre (see page 31).

**Swerve** An extreme amount of sidespin applied to the cue ball to make its path curve. This shot is most often used to escape from snookers; it is not easy to control.

47

# Useful addresses

## British Isles

The Billiards and Snooker
  Control Council
Coronet House
Queen Street
Leeds  LS1 2TN

Republic of Ireland Billiards and
  Snooker Association
3 Field Avenue
Walkintown
Dublin 12

Welsh Billiards and Snooker Association
69 Roman Way
Neath
West Glamorgan  SA10 7BH

Northern Ireland Billiards and
  Snooker Control Council
105 Glenburn Road
Dunmurry  BT17 9AR

Scottish Billiards and Snooker
  Association
17 Stockwell Street
Glasgow  ML5 5LQ

## Overseas

Australia Billiards and Snooker
  Association
PO Box 417
Spring Hill
Queensland 4004

Canada Billiards and Snooker
  Association
PO Box 1252
Saint John
New Brunswick  E2L 4G7

New Zealand Billiards and Snooker Association
Box 603
New Plymouth

## International

International Billiards and Snooker Federation
Coronet House
Queen Street
Leeds  LS1 2TN
United Kingdom

The IBSF is the world governing body, responsible for the rules
of snooker; the national governing bodies listed above are
among those affiliated to it.